WRIGHT FAMILY
BIRTH RECORDS, 1853 TO 1896
AND MARRIAGE RECORDS, 1782 TO 1900
IN
CAMPBELL COUNTY, VIRGINIA

Robert N. Grant

HERITAGE BOOKS
2011

HERITAGE BOOKS
AN IMPRINT OF HERITAGE BOOKS, INC.

Books, CDs, and more—Worldwide

For our listing of thousands of titles see our website
at
www.HeritageBooks.com

Published 2011 by
HERITAGE BOOKS, INC.
Publishing Division
100 Railroad Ave. #104
Westminster, Maryland 21157

International Standard Book Numbers
Paperbound: 978-0-7884-2563-9
Clothbound: 978-0-7884-8786-6

WRIGHT FAMILY

BIRTH RECORDS

CAMPBELL COUNTY, VIRGINIA

1853 TO 1896

Revised as of February 9, 2004

This document is an appendix to a larger work titled Sorting Some Of The Wrights Of Southern Virginia. The work is divided into parts for each family of Wrights that has been researched. Each part is divided into two sections; the first section is text discussing the family and the evidence supporting the relationships and the second section is a descendants chart summarizing the relationships and information known about each individual.

The appendices to the work (of which this document is one) present source records for persons named Wright by county and by type of record with the identification of the person named and their Wright ancestors to the extent known.

The source for the records listed in this appendix is the following:

1)   Campbell County, Virginia, Birth Records, available from The Library of Virginia, 11th at Capitol, Richmond, Virginia 23219.

The identification of a person or their ancestor by year and county indicates their year of death and county of residence at death. For example, "1763 Thomas Wright of Bedford County" indicates that this was the Thomas Wright who died in 1763 in Bedford County. If no state is listed after the county, the state is Virginia; counties in states other than Virginia will have a state listed after the county, as in "1876 William S. Wright of Highland County, Ohio".

A parenthetical after the name indicates an identification of the person when a place of death is not yet known, as in "John Wright (Goochland County Carpenter)". A county in parentheses after the name indicates the county with which that person was most identified when no evidence of the place of death has yet been found, as in "Grief Wright (Bedford County)".

All or portions of the text and descendants charts for each Wright family identified are available from the author:

Robert N. Grant
15 Campo Bello Court
Menlo Park, California 94025

(H) 650-854-0895
(O) 650-614-3800

This is a work in process and I would be most interested in receiving additional information about any of the persons identified in these records in order to correct any errors or expand on the information given.

Appendix: Campbell County, Virginia, Birth Records

Date	Name of Child	Other Information	Identification
1853/12/10	Ro. C. Wright	Color: White Sex: Male Born: Alive Place of Birth: Campbell Cy Va Father's Name: M P, B, or R Wright Father's Occupation: Farmer Father's Residence: Campbell Cy Va Mother's Name: Mary L. Wright How many: 1 Informant: M. P, B, or R Wright Relationship: Father	
1854/04/25	Benj F Wright	Color: White Sex: Male Born: Alive Place of Birth: Campbell Cy Father's Name: Thos B. Wright Father's Occupation: Carpenter Father's Residence: Campbell Mother's Name: Elizt A. Wright Informant: Eliz. A. Wright Relationship: Mother	Benjamin F. Wright, son of 1882 Thomas B. Wright of Campbell County and grandson of Thomas Wright (Campbell County)
1854/09/13	Jesse T. Wright	Color: White Sex: Male Born: Alive Place of Birth: Campbell Cy Father's Name: Jno P. Wright Sen Father's Occupation: Mechanic Father's Residence: Campbell Cy Mother's Name: Elizt Wright How many: 1 Informant: J P Wright Sen Relationship: Father	Jesse Hughes Wright, son of 1873 John Patterson Wright of Campbell County, grandson of 1811 John Wright of Campbell County, and great grandson of Robert Wright, Sr. (Campbell County)

Date	Name of Child	Other Information	Identification
1860/03/30	Horace M Wright	Color: White Sex: Male Place of Birth: Campbell Father's Name: J. W. Wright Father's Occupation: Constable Father's Residence: Campbell Mother's Name: Amanda M. Wright How many: 1 Informant: J. W. Wright Relationship: Father	Horace M. Wright, son of James W. Wright and grandson of 1860 Lewis Wright of Lynchburg
1864/11/00	Robt H. Wright	Color: White Sex: Male Born: Alive Place of Birth: Campbell Cy Father's Name: Tho. S. Wright Father's Occupation: Farmer Father's Residence: Campbell Mother's Name: Elizt Wright How many: 1 Informant: Tho. S. Wright Relationship: Father	Robert H. Wright, son of 1883 Thomas Smith Wright of Campbell County and grandson of 1842 Thomas Wright of Buckingham County
1866/06/14	Cornelia F Wright	Color: Colored Sex: Female Born: Alive Place of Birth: Campbell Father's Name: Nelson Wright Father's Occupation: Farmer Father's Residence: Campbell Mother's Name: Sarah Jane Wright How many: 1 Informant: Nelson Wright Relationship: Father	Cornelia F. Wright, daughter of Nelson Wright

Appendix: Campbell County, Virginia, Birth Records

Date	Name of Child	Other Information	Identification
1866/09/06	Ro. L Wright	Color: White Sex: Male Born: Alive Place of Birth: Campbell Father's Name: Jas W Wright Father's Occupation: Farmer Father's Residence: Campbell Mother's Name: Amand M Wright How many: 1 Informant: J W Wright Relationship: Father	Robert L. Wright, son of James W. Wright and grandson of 1860 Lewis Wright of Lynchburg
1871/11/21	Wm. Wright	Color: White Sex: Male Born: Alive Place of Birth: Campbell County Father's Name: Silas Wright Father's Occupation: Blacksmith Father's Residence: Campbell Mother's Name: Ann Wright How many: 1 Informant: Silas Wright Relationship: Head of Family	William Wright, son of Silas Wright
1874/02/01	J. R. Wright	Color: White Sex: Male Born: Alive Place of Birth: Campbell Father's Name: Sterling Wright Father's Occupation: Farmer Father's Residence: Campbell Mother's Name: Lucy A Wright How many: 1 Informant: L. A. Wright Relationship: Mother	J. R. Wright, son of Sterling Charles Wright, grandson of 1873 Robert D. Wright of Amherst County, great grandson of Charles Wright, and great great grandson of Robert Wright, Sr. (Campbell County)

Date	Name of Child	Other Information	Identification
1874/03/27	S. A K Wright	Color: Colored Sex: Female Born: Alive Place of Birth: Campbell Mother's Name: Sarah Wright How many: 1 Informant: S Wright Relationship: Mother	
1874/05/01	Alice Wright	Color: White Sex: Female Born: Alive Place of Birth: Campbell Father's Name: David L Wright Father's Occupation: Miller Father's Residence: Campbell Mother's Name: A. B Wright How many: 1 Informant: D L Wright Relationship: Father	Alice Wright, daughter of 1879 David Luther Wright, granddaughter of 1873 John Patterson Wright of Campbell County, great granddaughter of 1811 John Wright of Campbell County, and great great granddaughter of Robert Wright, Sr. (Campbell County)
1874/10/09	Lenard Wright	Color: Colored Sex: Male Born: Alive Place of Birth: Campbell Father's Name: Henry Wright Father's Occupation: Laborer Father's Residence: Campbell Mother's Name: Fanny Wright How many: 1 Informant: H. Wright Relationship: Father	Lenard Wright, son of Henry Wright

Appendix: Campbell County, Virginia, Birth Records

Date	Name of Child	Other Information	Identification
1874/11/20	James Edgar Wright	Color: White Sex: Male Born: Alive Place of Birth: Brookneal Campbell Father's Name: John E. Wright Father's Occupation: Tobacconist Father's Residence: Brookneal C. Mother's Name: Mary Wright How many: 1 Informant: James E Wright Relationship: Parent	James Edgar Wright, son of John E. Wright
1874/12/08	Rosa E. Wright	Color: White Sex: Female Born: Alive Place of Birth: Campbell Father's Name: Frank P. Wright Father's Occupation: Farmer Father's Residence: Campbell Mother's Name: Emma Wright How many: 1 Informant: F. P. Wright Relationship: Father	Rosa E. Wright, daughter of Franklin Pierce Wright, granddaughter of 1883 Thomas Smith Wright of Campbell County, and great granddaughter of 1842 Thomas Wright of Buckingham County
1876/08/13	James T Wright	Color: White Sex: Male Born: Alive Place of Birth: Campbell County Father's Name: John J Wright Father's Occupation: Farmer Father's Residence: Campbell Mother's Name: Susan E Wright How many: 1 Deformity: None Informant: S E Wright Relationship: Mother	James Thomas Wright, son of John James Wright, grandson of 1883 Thomas Smith Wright of Campbell County, and great grandson of 1842 Thomas Wright of Buckingham County

Date	Name of Child	Other Information	Identification
1877/02/08	Warren Wright	Color: White Sex: Male Place of Birth: Campbell Father's Name: David L Wright Father's Occupation: Farmer Father's Residence: Campbell Mother's Name: Alice Wright How many: 1 Deformity: None Informant: A. Wright Relationship: Mother	Warren Wright, son of 1879 David Luther Wright, grandson of 1873 John Patterson Wright of Campbell County, great grandson of 1811 John Wright of Campbell County, and great great grandson of Robert Wright, Sr. (Campbell County)
1878/02/08	Mary Wright	Color: White Sex: Female Born: Alive Place of Birth: Campbell Father's Name: S A Wright Mother's Name: Elizabeth Wright How many: 1 Deformity: None Informant: S A Wright Relationship: Father	Mary Jane (Wright) Kent, daughter of Samuel Anderson Wright, granddaughter of 1873 John Patterson Wright of Campbell County, great granddaughter of 1811 John Wright of Campbell County, and great great granddaughter of Robert Wright, Sr. (Campbell County)
1878/03/06	Edwin Wright	Color: White Sex: Male Born: Alive Place of Birth: Campbell Co Father's Name: Jesse H Wright Father's Occupation: Farmer Father's Residence: Campbell Mother's Name: Fannie Wright How many: 1 Deformity: None Informant: Jesse H Wright Relationship: Father	Edwin Wright, son of Jesse Hughes Wright, grandson of 1873 John Patterson Wright of Campbell County, great grandson of 1811 John Wright of Campbell County, and great great grandson of Robert Wright, Sr. (Campbell County)

Appendix: Campbell County, Virginia, Birth Records

Date	Name of Child	Other Information	Identification
1878/03/10	Emma H Wright	Color: Colored Sex: Female Place of Birth: Campbell Co Father's Name: Nelson Wright Father's Occupation: Farmer Father's Residence: Campbell Co Mother's Name: Clara E Wright How many: 1 Deformity: None Informant: Nelson Wright Relationship: Father	Emma H. Wright, daughter of Nelson Wright
1878/07/26	Hattie May Wright	Color: White Sex: Female Born: Alive Place of Birth: Campbell Co Father's Name: Thos T Wright Father's Occupation: Farmer Father's Residence: Campbell Mother's Name: Roberta H Wright How many: 1 Deformity: None Informant: Thos T Wright Relationship: Father	Hattie May or Addie Wright, daughter of Thomas Turner Wright, granddaughter of 1883 Thomas Smith Wright of Campbell County, and great granddaughter of 1842 Thomas Wright of Buckingham County
1878/10/10	____ Wright	Color: Colored Sex: Male Born: Alive Place of Birth: Campbell Co Father's Name: Richd Wright Father's Occupation: Farmer Father's Residence: Campbell Mother's Name: Fannie Wright How many: 1 Deformity: None Informant: Richd Wright Relationship: Father	

Date	Name of Child	Other Information	Identification
1879/08/01	____ Wright	Color: White Sex: Male Born: Alive Place of Birth: Campbell Co Father's Name: Wm R Wright Father's Occupation: Farmer Father's Residence: Campbell Mother's Name: Chestina W Wright How many: 1 Deformity: None Informant: Wm R Wright Relationship: Father	Daughter of William Richard Wright, granddaughter of 1882 Thomas B. Wright of Campbell County, and great granddaughter of Thomas Wright (Campbell County)
1880/03/00	Bessie Wright	Color: White Sex: Female Born: Alive Place of Birth: Brice Island Father's Name: David Wright Father's Occupation: Farmer Father's Residence: Campbell County Mother's Name: Alice Wright How many: 1 Deformity: None Informant: David Wright Relationship: Father	Bessie Wright, daughter of 1879 David Luther Wright, granddaughter of 1873 John Patterson Wright of Campbell County, great granddaughter of 1811 John Wright of Campbell County, and great great granddaughter of Robert Wright, Sr. (Campbell County)
1880/09/05	Effie L Wright	Color: White Sex: Female Born: Alive Place of Birth: Campbell County Father's Name: Thos T Wright Father's Occupation: Farmer Father's Residence: Campbell County Mother's Name: Roberta H Wright How many: 1 Deformity: None Informant: Thos T Wright Relationship: Father	Effie L. Wright, daughter of Thomas Turner Wright, granddaughter of 1883 Thomas Smith Wright of Campbell County, and great granddaughter of 1842 Thomas Wright of Buckingham County

Appendix: Campbell County, Virginia, Birth Records

Date	Name of Child	Other Information	Identification
1881/03/06	Bessie Wright	Color: White Sex: Female Born: Alive Place of Birth: Campbell County Father's Name: David Wright Father's Occupation: Farmer Father's Residence: Campbell County Mother's Name: Alice Wright How many: 1 Deformity: None Informant: David Wright Relationship: Father	Bessie Wright, daughter of 1879 David Luther Wright, granddaughter of 1873 John Patterson Wright of Campbell County, great granddaughter of 1811 John Wright of Campbell County, and great great granddaughter of Robert Wright, Sr. (Campbell County) [apparently listed twice]
1881/08/22	Grace T. Wright	Color: White Sex: Female Born: Alive Place of Birth: Campbell County Father's Name: James R Wright Father's Occupation: Farmer Father's Residence: Campbell County Mother's Name: Jane R Wright How many: 1 Deformity: None Informant: James P. Wright Relationship: Father	Grace T. Wright, daughter of James Robert Wright, granddaughter of 1882 Thomas B. Wright of Campbell County, and great granddaughter of Thomas Wright (Campbell County)
1881/11/01	Edgar P Wright	Color: White Sex: Male Born: Alive Place of Birth: Campbell County Father's Name: John J Wright Father's Occupation: Farmer Father's Residence: Campbell County Mother's Name: Susan Wright How many: 1 Deformity: None Informant: John J Wright Relationship: Father	Edgar P. Wright, son of John James Wright, grandson of 1883 Thomas Smith Wright of Campbell County, and great grandson of 1842 Thomas Wright of Buckingham County

Appendix: Campbell County, Virginia, Birth Records

Date	Name of Child	Other Information	Identification
1884/12/06	Elizabeth A Wright	Color: White Sex: Female Born: Alive Place of Birth: Campbell County Father's Name: Benj F Wright Father's Occupation: Farmer Father's Residence: Campbell County Mother's Name: Sarah E Wright How many: 1 Deformity: None Informant: Benj F Wright Relationship: Father	Elizabeth A. Wright, daughter of Benjamin F. Wright, granddaughter of 1882 Thomas B. Wright of Campbell County, and great granddaughter of Thomas Wright (Campbell County)
1888/02/27	Taswell M. Wright	Color: White Sex: Male Born: Alive Place of Birth: Campbell County Father's Name: Jas. R. Wright Father's Occupation: Farm Laborer Father's Residence: Campbell County Mother's Name: Jane T. Wright How many: 1 Deformity: None Informant: J. R. Wright Relationship: Father	Taswell M. Wright, son of James Robert Wright, grandson of 1882 Thomas B. Wright of Campbell County, and great grandson of Thomas Wright (Campbell County)
1888/10/15	Kate Wright	Color: Colored Sex: Female Born: Alive Place of Birth: Campbell County Mother's Name: Jenny Wright How many: 1 Deformity: None Informant: Kiah Ford Relationship: Friend	

Appendix: Campbell County, Virginia, Birth Records

Date	Name of Child	Other Information	Identification
1888/12/08	_____ Wright	Color: Colored Sex: Male Born: Alive Place of Birth: Campbell County Father's Name: Benj. Wright Father's Occupation: Farm Laborer Father's Residence: Campbell County Mother's Name: Molly Wright How many: 1 Deformity: None Informant: B. Wright Relationship: Father	
1890/01/30	Edwd H. Wright	Color: White Sex: Male Born: Alive Place of Birth: Campbell County Father's Name: Jas. R. Wright Father's Occupation: Farmer Father's Residence: Campbell County Mother's Name: Jane F. Wright How many: 1 Deformity: None Informant: J. R. Wright Relationship: Father	Edward H. Wright, son of James Robert Wright, grandson of 1882 Thomas B. Wright of Campbell County, and great grandson of Thomas Wright (Campbell County)
1890/10/10	Martha E. Wright	Color: Colored Sex: Female Born: Alive Place of Birth: Campbell County Mother's Name: Mennie Wright How many: 1 Deformity: None Informant: Jordan Elliott Relationship: Friend	

Date	Name of Child	Other Information	Identification
1890/11/03	Mary E. Wright	Color: White Sex: Female Born: Alive Place of Birth: Campbell County Father's Name: Benj F. Wright Father's Occupation: Carpenter Father's Residence: Campbell County Mother's Name: Sarah E. Wright How many: 1 Deformity: None Informant: B. F. Wright Relationship: Father	Mary E. Wright, daughter of Benjamin F. Wright, granddaughter of 1882 Thomas B. Wright of Campbell County, and great granddaughter of Thomas Wright (Campbell County)
1891/02/17	Kate Wright	Color: Colored Sex: Female Born: Alive Place of Birth: Campbell County Father's Name: Beauregard Wright Father's Occupation: Miller Father's Residence: Campbell Co. Mother's Name: Nannie Wright How many: 1 Deformity: None Informant: B Wright Relationship: Father	Kate Wright, daughter of Beauregard Wright
1891/08/23	Rosa B. Wright	Color: White Sex: Female Born: Alive Place of Birth: Campbell County Father's Name: Jno A Wright Father's Occupation: Laborer Father's Residence: Campbell Co. Mother's Name: Sallie A. Wright How many: 1 Deformity: None Informant: J. A Wright Relationship: Father	Rosa B. Wright, daughter of John H. Wright, granddaughter of 1882 Thomas B. Wright of Campbell County, and great granddaughter of Thomas Wright (Campbell County)

Appendix: Campbell County, Virginia, Birth Records

Date	Name of Child	Other Information	Identification
1891/10/10	Myrtle Wright	Color: White Sex: Female Born: Alive Place of Birth: Campbell County Father's Name: Tho. T. Wright Father's Occupation: Farmer Father's Residence: Campbell Co Mother's Name: R. H. Wright How many: 1 Deformity: None Informant: T. T. Wright Relationship: Father	Myrtle Wright, daughter of Thomas Turner Wright, granddaughter of 1883 Thomas Smith Wright of Campbell County, and great granddaughter of 1842 Thomas Wright of Buckingham County
1891/11/03	Mary E Wright	Color: White Sex: Male Born: Alive Place of Birth: Campbell Father's Name: Ben F Wright Father's Occupation: Laborer Father's Residence: Campbell Mother's Name: Sarah E Write How many: 1 Deformity: No deformity Informant: Parents	Mary E. Wright, daughter of Benjamin F. Wright, granddaughter of 1882 Thomas B. Wright of Campbell County, and great granddaughter of Thomas Wright (Campbell County)
1892/02/26	Wm Richard Wright	Color: White Sex: Male Born: Alive Place of Birth: Campbell Co. Father's Name: James Wright Father's Occupation: Farmer Father's Residence: Campbell Mother's Name: Jennie R Wright How many: 1 Deformity: No Deformity Informant: Jas Wright Relationship: Parent	William Richard Wright, son of James Robert Wright, grandson of 1882 Thomas B. Wright of Campbell County, and great grandson of Thomas Wright (Campbell County)

Date	Name of Child	Other Information	Identification
1893/07/16	Minnie M Wright	Color: White Sex: Female Born: Alive Place of Birth: Campbell Co Va Father's Name: Ben L Wright Father's Occupation: Carpenter Father's Residence: Campbell Mother's Name: Sarah E Wright How many: 1 Deformity: No deformity Informant: B L Wright Relationship: Parent	Minnie M. Wright, daughter of Benjamin F. Wright, granddaughter of 1882 Thomas B. Wright of Campbell County, and great granddaughter of Thomas Wright (Campbell County)
1894/10/20	Harry W. Wright	Color: White Sex: Male Born: Alive Place of Birth: Campbell County Father's Name: Tho. T. Wright Father's Occupation: Farmer Father's Residence: Campbell Co Mother's Name: Roberta H. Wright How many: 1 Deformity: None Informant: T. T. Wright Relationship: Father	Harry W. Wright, son of Thomas Turner Wright, grandson of 1883 Thomas Smith Wright of Campbell County and great grandson of 1842 Thomas Wright of Buckingham County
1895/05/25	Nannie Wright	Color: Colored Sex: Female Born: Alive Place of Birth: Near Tyreanna Father's Name: Beauregard Wright Father's Occupation: Miller Father's Residence: Near Tyreanna Mother's Name: Nannie Wright How many: 1 Informant: Nannie Wright Relationship: Mother	Nannie Wright, daughter of Beauregard Wright

Appendix: Campbell County, Virginia, Birth Records

Date	Name of Child	Other Information	Identification
1895/10/29	Adelade Wright	Color: White Sex: Female Born: Alive Place of Birth: White R. Hill Father's Name: Edward S. Wright Father's Occupation: Com. Laborer Father's Residence: White R Hill Mother's Name: Nannie Wright How many: 1 Informant: Nannie Wright Relationship: Mother	Adelaide Wright, daughter of Edward Sylvanus Wright, granddaughter of John H. Wright, great granddaughter of 1882 Thomas B. Wright of Campbell County, and great great granddaughter of Thomas Wright (Campbell County)
1896/03/26	Chas Henry Wright	Color: White Sex: Male Born: Alive Place of Birth: Southern R.R. Father's Name: Benj. F. Wright Father's Occupation: Carpenter Father's Residence: Southern R.R. Mother's Name: Sarah E. Wright How many: 1 Informant: Benj. F. Wright Relationship: Father	Charles Henry Wright, son of Benjamin F. Wright, grandson of 1882 Thomas B. Wright of Campbell County, and great grandson of Thomas Wright (Campbell County)
1896/08/07	Nettie May Wright	Color: White Sex: Female Born: Alive Place of Birth: L. & O. R.R. Father's Name: Wartie B. Wright Father's Occupation: Farmer Father's Residence: L & O. R.R. Mother's Name: Sarah E. Wright How many: 1 Informant: Wartie B. Wright Relationship: Father	Nettie May Wright, daughter of Wartie B. Wright

INDEX

WRIGHT FAMILY

MARRIAGE RECORDS

CAMPBELL COUNTY, VIRGINIA

1782 TO 1900

Revised as of February 9, 2004

This document is an appendix to a larger work titled Sorting Some Of The Wrights Of Southern Virginia. The work is divided into parts for each family of Wrights that has been researched. Each part is divided into two sections; the first section is text discussing the family and the evidence supporting the relationships and the second section is a descendants chart summarizing the relationships and information known about each individual.

The appendices to the work (of which this document is one) present source records for persons named Wright by county and by type of record with the identification of the person named and their Wright ancestors to the extent known.

The sources for the records listed in this appendix are the following:

1) Campbell County, Virginia, Marriage Records, available from the Clerk of the Circuit Court, P.O. Box 7, Rustburg, Virginia 24588.

2) Marriages of Campbell County, Virginia 1782-1810, by Lucy Baber and Hazel Williamson, Lynchburg, Virginia, 1971.

3) Campbell County, Virginia, Marriage Bonds 1781-1854, by Genealogical Society of Utah, 1937.

The identification of a person or their ancestor by year and county indicates their year of death and county of residence at death. For example, "1763 Thomas Wright of Bedford County" indicates that this was the Thomas Wright who died in 1763 in Bedford County. If no state is listed after the county, the state is Virginia; counties in states other than Virginia will have a state listed after the county, as in "1876 William S. Wright of Highland County, Ohio"

A parenthetical after the name indicates an identification of the person when a place of death is not yet known, as in "John Wright (Goochland County Carpenter)". A county in parentheses after the name indicates the county with which that person was most identified when no evidence of the place of death has yet been found, as in "Grief Wright (Bedford County)".

All or portions of the text and descendants charts for each Wright family identified are available from the author:

Robert N. Grant
15 Campo Bello Court   (H) 650-854-0895
Menlo Park, California 94025   (O) 650-614-3800

This is a work in progress and I would be most interested in receiving additional information about any of the persons identified in these records in order to correct any errors or expand on the information given.

Appendix: Campbell County, Virginia, Marriage Records

Book/Page		Date	Names	Other Information	Identification
01	181	1791/11/03	Robert Wright & Rachel Paxton	Daughter of William & Mary Betts Surety: Henry Williamson Witness: Henry Williamson Witness: John Paxson Married by: William Dameron	1829 Robert Wright of Knox County, Ohio, son of 1818 Anthony Wright of Loudoun County
		1798/00/21	Robert Wright & Frances Staples	Married by: William Flowers	1815 Robert C. Wright of Prince Edward County, son of 1820 Pryor Wright, Sr., of Prince Edward County and grandson of 1779 John Wright of Prince Edward County
01	181	1798/10/20	Robert Wright & Anna or Anne Doss	Surety: John Rector Witness: Charles Wright Witness: John Rector	Robert Wright, Jr., son of Robert Wright, Sr. (Campbell County)
01	018	1800/01/13	William Burnett & Susanna Wright	Consent of Susanna Wright Witness: Robert Wright Witness: Charles Wright Surety: Robert Wright	Susanna (Wright) Burnett, probably daughter of Robert Wright, Sr. (Campbell County)
01	065	1800/04/23	Perrin Giles & Elizabeth Wright	Consent of Elizabeth Wright who is of age Witness: Robert Wright Witness: Anny Wright Surety: Robert Wright	Elizabeth (Wright) Giles, daughter of Robert Wright, Sr. (Campbell County)
01	181	1802/03/08	George Wright & Agnes Doss	Consent of Agness Doss who is of full age Witness: Jacob Golding Witness: David Elliott Surety: Jacob Golding	1823 George Wright of Campbell County, son of Robert Wright, Sr. (Campbell County)
01	181	1806/01/13	John Wright & Martha Guttery	Daughter of James Guttery Witness: Henry Guttery Witness: John Candler Surety: Henry Candler	

Book/Page	Date	Names	Other Information	Identification
	1806/10/09	Robert Wright & Polley Godsey	Daughter of Molley Godsey Witness: Joseph Tweedy, Jr. Witness: Archer Williamson Surety: Archer Williamson	1818 Robert "Robin" Wright of Campbell County, son of 1805 Thomas Wright of Campbell County and grandson of 1779 John Wright of Prince Edward County
01 181	1808/10/10	Robert Wright, Sr. & Kezia Gilinwaters	Witness: Thomas Jones Surety: Thomas Jones	Robert Wright, Sr. (Campbell County)
01 163	1809/05/31	James Turner & Eliza Wright	Daughter of Sylvia Wright Witness: Polly Wright Witness: Rob Wright Surety: Robert Wright	Eliza (Wright) Turner, daughter of 1805 Thomas Wright of Campbell County and granddaughter of 1779 John Wright of Prince Edward County
01 005	1814/04/20	Tarlton W. Askew or Asher & Polly Wright	Daughter of Chas. Wright Witness: John Asher Jr. Witness: James D. Cardwell Witness: Tho. Mitchell Jr. Surety James D. Cardwell	Polly (Wright) Askew or Asher, daughter of Charles Wright and granddaughter of Robert Wright, Sr. (Campbell County)
01 181	1821/06/19	George A. Wright & Mildred Plunkett	Declaration of Daniel Stratton as of age Witness: Daniel P. Wright Surety: Daniel P. Wright	1879 George Anderson Wright, son of 1811 John Wright of Campbell County and grandson of Robert Wright, Sr. (Campbell County)
01 058	1821/10/09	John Foster & Elizabeth Wright	Daughter of Charles Wright Witness: William P. Wright Surety: William P. Wright	Elizabeth (Wright) Foster, daughter of Charles Wright and granddaughter of Robert Wright, Sr. (Campbell County)
01 003	1822/11/14	John Alvis & Sally Wright	Daughter of George Wright, deceased Consent of Agnes Wright Surety: John Walker, Jr.	Sally M. (Wright) Alvis, daughter of 1823 George Wright of Campell County and granddaughter of Robert Wright, Sr. (Campbell County)
01 181	1823/08/28	John P. Wright & Nancy P. Mathews	Daughter of Phillip Mathews Witness: Leroy Davidson Witness Daniel Davidson Surety: Leroy Davidson	1873 John Patterson Wright of Campbell County, son of 1811 John Wright of Campbell County and grandson of Robert Wright, Sr. (Campbell County)

Appendix: Campbell County, Virginia, Marriage Records

Book/Page		Date	Names	Other Information	Identification
01	181	1823/09/30	Pryor B. Wright & Lucinda Wright	Consent of Lucinda P. Wright as of age Witness: Parker A. Wright Witness: Creek Jenkins Surety Parker A. Wright	1882 Pryor B. Wright of Appomattox County, son of 1854 Samuel A. Wright of Appomattox County, grandson of 1820 Pryor Wright, Sr., of Prince Edward County, and great grandson of 1779 John Wright of Prince Edward County and Lucinda P. (Wright) Wright, daughter of 1815 Robert C. Wright of Prince Edward County, granddaughter of 1820 Pryor Wright of Prince Edward County, and great granddaughter of 1779 John Wright of Prince Edward County
01	181	1825/11/21	Pryor Wright & Mariah Turner	Daughter of Leonard Turner Witness: ____ Jenkins Witness: ____ Turner Surety: John Turner	1854 Pryor Rucker Wright, Jr. of Appomattox County, son of 1820 Pryor Wright, Sr., of Prince Edward County and grandson of 1779 John Wright of Prince Edward County
01	181	1825/11/29	Wilson Wright & Elizabeth Maberry	Daughter of William Maberry Witness: John Maberry Surety: William. Maberry	Wilson M. Wright, son of 1823 George Wright of Campbell County and granddaughter of Robert Wright, Sr. (Campbell County)
01	181	1826/09/12	Elijah A. Wright & Elizabeth Bowley or Boley	Witness: Jonathan Bailey Witness: Jonathan Martin Witness: Charlotte Boley Surety: Jonathan Martin	Elijah A. Wright, son of 1811 John Wright of Campbell County and grandson of Robert Wright, Sr. (Campbell County)
01	181	1830/02/03	John H. Wright & Elizabeth Wilson	Daughter of John Wilson Witness: Peter H. Wilson Surety: Peter H. Wilson	1849 John H. Wright of Bedford County, son of 1810 John Wright of Bedford County and grandson of 1767 Francis Wright of Amherst County
01	181	1832/08/22	Thomas B. Wright & Elizabeth A. Wood	Daughter of Joseph Wood Witness: William G. H. Bingham Surety: William G. H. Bingham	1882 Thomas B. Wright of Campbell County, son of Thomas Wright (Campbell County)
01	181	1833/12/18	Robert C. Wright & Sarah Johnson	Daughter of Philip Johnson Witness: Daniel Stratton Witness: Vallentine Gillinwaters Surety: Vallentine Gillinwaters	
01	181	1835/02/16	Meredith P. Wright & Mary L. Williams	Daughter of William Williams Witness: Thomas A. Woodson Surety: Thomas A. Woodson	Meredith P. Wright, son of 1823 George Wright of Campbell County and granddaughter of Robert Wright, Sr. (Campbell County)

Book/Page		Date	Names	Other Information	Identification
01	182	1840/03/04	John P. Wright & Elizabeth Hughes	Daughter of John Hughes Witness: John Caves Witness: Saml. G. Martin Surety: Saml. G. Martin	1873 John Patterson Wright of Campbell County, son of 1811 John Wright of Campbell County ard grandson of Robert Wright, Sr. (Campbell County)
01	182	1842/03/29	Lovin A. Wright & Elizabeth Ann Martin	Daughter of John Martin Witness: Frances A. J. Calley Witness: Jas. B. Durrum Surety: James B. Durrum	Loving A. Wright, son of 1854 Samuel A. Wright of Appomattox County, grandson of 1820 Pryor Wright, Sr. of Prince Edward County, and great grandson of 1779 John Wright of Prince Edward County
01	182	1843/09/05	Robert J. Wright & Frances Colley	Witness: Wm. W. G. Durrum Witness: Wm. M. Wright Witness: Fanetta R. Durrum Surety: Wm. M. Wright	Robert J. Wright, probably son of 1854 Samuel A. Wright of Appomattox County, grandson of 1820 Pryor Wright, Sr., of Prince Edward County, and great grandson of 1779 John Wright of Prince Edward County
01	182	1846/02/18	Campbell S. Wright & Mildred Ann Durrium	Widow Jame B. Durrium, deceased Witness: Robert B. Wright Surety: Robert B. Wright	Campbell S. Wright, son of 1854 Pryor Rucker Wright, Jr., of Appomattox County, grandson of 1820 Pryor Wright, Sr. of Prince Edward County, and great grandson of 1779 John Wright of Prince Edward County
01	182	1848/12/18	Elisha F. Wright & Lucy Ann Johnson	Daughter of Patrick Johnson Witness: George A. Wright Witness: Camden G. Wright Surety: Camden G. Wright	
02	016	1852/11/27	George A. Wright & Amanda Smith	Wife's Par: Paschel Smith	George Alexander Wright, son of 1823 George Wright of Campbell County and grandson of Robert Wright, Sr. (Campbell County)
02	018	1853/03/23	Samuel J. Hodges & Sarah E. Wright	Daughter of John B. Wright Witness: Richard ____ Witness: Moses Glass Surety: John B. Wright	

Appendix: Campbell County, Virginia, Marriage Records

Book/Page		Date	Names	Other Information	Identification
02	037	1857/01/20	James W. Wright & Amanda M. Walthall	Place: Wm C Perrow Husb's Age: 28 Wife's Age: 24 Husb's Cond: Single Wife's Cond: Single Husb Born: Amherst, Va Wife Born: Campbell Husb's Res: Bedford Wife's Res: Campbell Husb's Par: Lewis & Elizabeth Wife's Par: Robert Walthall & Betsy Ann Husb's Occupation: Constable & Farmer	James W. Wright, son of 1860 Lewis Wright of Lynchburg
02	041	1857/12/01	George D. Blanks & Nannie M. Wright	Wife's Par: John P. Wright	Nancy M. (Wright) Blanks, daughter of 1873 John Patterson Wright of Campbell County, granddaughter of 1811 John Wright of Campbell County, and great granddaughter of Robert Wright, Sr. (Campbell County)
02	042	1858/01/05	Robert D. Wright & Margaret A. Mason	Place: Campbell County Va Husb's Age: 21 Wife's Age: 21 Husb's Cond: Single Wife's Cond: Single Husb Born: Amherst Co. Va. Wife Born: Charlotte Co. Va. Husb's Res: Amherst Co. Va Wife's Res: Campbell Co. Va Husb's Par: Robert & Ellen Wright Wife's Par: George W. & Parthenia R. Mason Husb's Occ: Blacksmith Minister: Geo W. Carter	Robert Doss Wright, son of 1873 Robert D. Wright of Amherst County, probably grandson of Charles Wright, and probably great grandson of Robert Wright, Sr. (Campbell County)

Book/Page	Date	Names	Other Information	Identification
02 088	1866/03/21	Fuller Johnson & Mary A. Wright	Place: Jno. Edds, Campbell Cy. Husb's Age: 24 Wife's Age: 27 Husb's Cond: single Wife's Cond: single Husb Born: Campbell Cy Va Wife Born: Campbell Cy Va Husb's Res: Campbell Cy Va Wife's Res: Campbell Cy Va Husb's Par: ___ & Sally Johnson Wife's Par: Tho. B. & ___ Wright Husb's Occ: Farmer Minister: James Austin	Mary A. (Wright) Johnson, daughter of 1882 Thomas B. Wright of Campbell County and granddaughter of Thomas Wright (Campbell County)
02 094	1866/12/27	Marion Coals & Eliza Wright	Witness: Austin Brooks	
02 098	1867/02/08	William R. Wright & Mrs. Chastina Dunnivant	Place: Mr James Mitchells Husb's Age: 30 Wife's Age: 32 Husb's Cond: single Wife's Cond: widowed Husb Born: Campbell Wife Born: Campbell Husb's Res: Campbell Wife's Res: Campbell Husb's Par: Tho. B & Elizabeth Wright Wife's Par: Paschal B & Nancy Smith Husb's Occ: Carpenter Minister: Joseph Spriggs	William R. Wright, son of 1882 Thomas B. Wright of Campbell County and grandson of Thomas Wright (Campbell County)

Appendix: Campbell County, Virginia, Marriage Records

Book/Page	Date	Names	Other Information	Identification
02 099	1867/03/15	James A. Wood & Catharine R. Wright	Place: Mr. Benj Woods Husb's Age: 21 Wife's Age: 23 Husb's Cond: single Wife's Cond: single Husb Born: Campbell Co Va Wife Born: Campbell Co Va Husb's Res: Campbell Co Va Wife's Res: Campbell Co Va Husb's Par: Wm B. & Martha A Wood Wife's Par: Thos B. & Betsy A. Wright Husb's Occ: Farmer Minister: Joseph Spriggs	Catharine R. (Wright) Wood, daughter of 1882 Thomas B. Wright of Campbell County and grandson of Thomas Wr ght (Campbell County)
02 113	1868/01/01	John J. Wright & Susan E. Litchford		John James Wright, son of 1883 Thomas Smith Wright of Campbell County and grandson of 1842 Thomas Wright of Buckingham County
02 123	1868/12/09	Benj. P. Wright & Delia E. Horton	Place: A G Hortons Husb's Age: 34 Wife's Age: Husb's Cond: Single Wife's Cond: Single Husb Born: Bedford Co. Va Wife Born: Campbell Co. Va Husb's Res: Bedford Co. Va Wife's Res: Campbell Co. Va Husb's Par: Price & Sarah Wright Wife's Par: A G & _ Horton Husb's Occ: Farmer Minister: Joseph Spriggs	Benjamin Price Wright, son of 1841 Price Wright of Bedford County, grandson of 1835 Benjamin Wright of Bedford County, great grandson of 1814 John Wright of Bedford County, and great great grandson of John Wright (Goochland County Carpenter)

Book/Page	Date	Names	Other Information	Identification
02 136	1869/06/16	W. H. Wright & Emma N. Pettigrew	Place: Bride's father's house Husb's Age: 29 Wife's Age: 23 Husb's Cond: Single Wife's Cond: Single Husb Born: Nelson Co Va. Wife Born: Botetourt Co Va. Husb's Res: Campbell Co Va. Wife's Res: Campbell Co Va. Husb's Par: Shelton & Paulina P. Wife's Par: James W. & Mary H Husb's Occ: Farmer Minister: George W. Langhorne	1914 William H. Wright of Bedford County, son of 1880 Shelton Wright, grandson of 1850 Jesse Wright of Nelson County, great grandson of 1799 Benjamin Wright of Amherst County, and great great grandson of 1767 Francis Wright of Amherst County
02 152	1870/08/21	Thomas J. Garvin & Elizabeth Wright	Place: Husb's Age: 52 Wife's Age: 37 Husb's Cond: widow Wife's Cond: Single Husb Born: Campbell Co. Wife Born: Campbell Co. Husb's Res: Campbell Co. Wife's Res: Campbell Co. Husb's Par: Alex: & Nancy Garvin Wife's Par: Danl & Eliz. Wright Husb's Occ: Farmer Minister: E. A. Gibbs	Elizabeth (Wright) Garvin, daughter of Daniel P. Wright, granddaughter of 1811 John Wright of Campbell County, and great granddaughter of Robert Wright, Sr. (Campbell County)

Appendix: Campbell County, Virginia, Marriage Records

Book/Page	Date	Names	Other Information	Identification
02 155	1870/12/28	Samuel F. Woodall & Bettie E. Wright	Place: Campbell County Husb's Age: 25 Wife's Age: 21 Husb's Cond: Single Wife's Cond: Single Husb Born: Campbell County Wife Born: Campbell County Husb's Res: Campbell County Wife's Res: Campbell County Husb's Par: Cyrus & Elizabeth Woodall Wife's Par: Elifat Wright Husb's Occ: Farmer Minister: Chas. A. Miles	Bettie E. (Wright) Woodall, daughter of Elifat Wright
02 164	1871/04/27	Robert R. Cardwell & Sallie Wright	Place: J. P. Wrights Husb's Age: 27 Wife's Age: 21 Husb's Cond: Single Wife's Cond: Single Husb Born: Campbell County Va. Wife Born: Campbell County Va. Husb's Res: Campbell County Va. Wife's Res: Campbell County Va. Husb's Par: Thos D. & Edney A. Wife's Par: J. P. & Elizabeth Husb's Occ: Farmer Minister:	Sallie Kit (Wright) Cardwell, daughter of 1873 John Patterson Wright of Campbell County, granddaughter of 1811 John Wright of Campbell County, and great granddaughter of Robert Wright, Sr. (Campbell County)

Appendix: Campbell County, Virginia, Marriage Records

Book/Page	Date	Names	Other Information	Identification
02 165	1871/11/21	J. C. Day & Elizabeth F. Wright	Place: Thos B. Wright Husb's Age: 22 Wife's Age: 18 Husb's Cond: Single Wife's Cond: Single Husb Born: Campbell County Va Wife Born: Campbell County Va Husb's Res: Campbell County Va Wife's Res: Campbell County Va Husb's Par: Danl. & Nancy Day Wife's Par: Thos B. & Betsy Ann Wright Husb's Occ: Farmer Minister: S. J. Liggan	Elizabeth F. (Wright) Day, daughter of 1882 Thomas B. Wright of Campbell County and granddaughter of Thomas Wright (Campbell County)
02 169	1872/12/18	Samuel A. Wright & Bettie M. Drinkard	Place: William Drinkards Husb's Age: 22 Wife's Age: 18 Husb's Cond: Single Wife's Cond: Single Husb Born: Campbell County Va Wife Born: Campbell County Va Husb's Res: Campbell County Va Wife's Res: Campbell County Va Husb's Par: John P & Betsy Wright Wife's Par: William & Mary Drinkard Husb's Occ: Cabinet Maker Minister: R. E. Booker	Samuel Anderson Wright, son of 1873 John Patterson Wright of Campbell County, grandson of 1811 John Wright of Campbell County, and great grandson of Robert Wright, Sr. (Campbell County)

Appendix: Campbell County, Virginia, Marriage Records

Book/Page	Date	Names	Other Information	Identification
02 170	1873/04/13	James R. Wright & M.C. Hendrick	Place: Lynchburg Va Col: White Husb's Age: 22 Wife's Age: 17 Husb's Cond: Single Wife's Cond: Single Husb Born: Campbell County Va Wife Born: Campbell County Va Husb's Res: Campbell County Va Wife's Res: Campbell County Va Husb's Par: Thos B. & Betsy Ann Wright Wife's Par: Husb's Occ: Farmer Minister: S. J. Liggan	James Robert Wright, son of 1882 Thomas B. Wright of Campbell County and grandson of Thomas Wright (Campbell County)
02 172	1873/12/24	George D. Drinkard & Mary A. Wright	Place: Rustburg Township Col: White Husb's Age: 26 Wife's Age: 28 Husb's Cond: single Wife's Cond: single Husb Born: Campbell County Va Wife Born: Campbell County Va Husb's Res: Campbell County Va Wife's Res: Campbell County Va Husb's Par: James & Lucy Drinkard Wife's Par: Jno P & Elizabeth Wright Husb's Occ: Farmer Minister: R. E. Booker	Mary Allen (Wright) Drinkard, daughter of 1873 John Patterson Wright of Campbell County, granddaughter of 1811 John Wright of Campbell County, and great granddaughter of Robert Wright, Sr. (Campbell County)

Book/Page	Date	Names	Other Information	Identification
02 173	1874/03/23	John C. Williams & Nannie J. Wright	Place: Falling Riv Township Col: White Husb's Age: 21 Wife's Age: 16 Husb's Cond: single Wife's Cond: single Husb Born: Appomattox Co Va Wife Born: Campbell Co Va Husb's Res: Appomattox Co Va Wife's Res: Campbell Co Va Husb's Par: J A. & A. C Williams Wife's Par: C. S. & M. A. Wright Husb's Occ: Farmer Minister: Thomas Fulton	Nannie C. or J. (Wright) Williams, daughter of Campbell S. Wright, granddaughter of 1854 Pryor Rucker Wright, Jr., of Appomattox County, great granddaughter of 1820 Pryor Wright, Sr., of Prince Edward County, and great great granddaughter of 1779 John Wright of Prince Edward County
02 063	1876/12/13	John W. Wright & Delia F. Layne	Place: Rustburg Mag. District Col: White Husb's Age: 26 Wife's Age: 18 Husb's Cond: single Wife's Cond: single Husb Born: Campbell Co. Va Wife Born: Campbell Co. Va Husb's Res: Campbell Co. Va Wife's Res: Campbell Co. Va Husb's Par: James & _ Wright William & Susan Wright Wife's Par: Jas. _ & E_beth Layne Husb's Occ: Farm_ Minister: J. T. Thornhill	John W. Wright, son of William Wesley Wright

Appendix: Campbell County, Virginia, Marriage Records

Book/Page	Date	Names	Other Information	Identification
02 064	1877/04/25	Jesse H. Wright & Blanche E. Cardwell	Place: Rustburg Mag. District Col: White Husb's Age: 22 Wife's Age: 18 Husb's Cond: single Wife's Cond: single Husb Born: Campbell Co. Va. Wife Born: Campbell Co. Va. Husb's Res: Campbell Co. Va. Wife's Res: Campbell Co. Va. Husb's Par: John P & Elizabeth Wright Wife's Par: Thos. D & Edney Cardwell Husb's Occ: Miller Minister: J. E. McSparrar	Jessie Hughes or Herbert Wright, son of 1873 John Patterson Wright of Campbell County, grandson of 1811 John Wright of Campbell County, and great grandson of Robert Wright, Sr. (Campbell County)
02 064	1877/09/11	James A. Wright & Blanch Hunt	Place: Brookville Mag District Col: White Husb's Age: 23 Wife's Age: 21 Husb's Cond: single Wife's Cond: single Husb Born: Campbell County Va Wife Born: Franklin County Va Husb's Res: Campbell County Va Wife's Res: Campbell County Va Husb's Par: James A & Elizabeth Wright Wife's Par: _ Hunt & Bell Tate Husb's Occ: Farmer Minister: W. S. Hall	James A. Wright, son of James A. Wright and grandson of William Wright (Buckingham County)

Book/Page	Date	Names	Other Information	Identification
02 067	1879/09/03	R. T. Martin & F. K. Wright	Place: Campbell Co Va Col: White Husb's Age: 36 Wife's Age: 30 Husb's Cond: single Wife's Cond: single Husb Born: Campbell Co Va Wife Born: Campbell Co Va Husb's Res: Campbell Co Va Wife's Res: Campbell Co Va Husb's Par: Jonathan & Nancy Martin Wife's Par: Thos S. & Elizabith Wright Husb's Occ: Farming Minister: Wm. P. Wright	Frances K. or Catherine (Wright) Martin, daughter of 1883 Thomas Smith Wright of Campbell County and granddaughter of 1842 Thomas Wright of Buckingham County
02 070	1880/02/26	James Robert Wright & Jane T. R. H. Trent	Place: Campbell Co Va Col: White Husb's Age: 28 Wife's Age: 18 Husb's Cond: widowed Wife's Cond: single Husb Born: Campbell Co Va Wife Born: Campbell Co Va Husb's Res: Campbell Co Va Wife's Res: Campbell Co Va Husb's Par: Thos & Betsy Ann Wright Wife's Par: Tazwell & Grace Trent Husb's Occ: Farming Minister: Jno. T. Rodes	James Robert Wright, son of 1882 Thomas B. Wright of Campbell County and grandson of Thomas Wright (Campbell County)

Appendix: Campbell County, Virginia, Marriage Records

Book/Page		Date	Names	Other Information	Identification
02	068	1881/03/30	Benjamin F. Wright & Sarah E. Trent	Place: Campbell Co Va Col: White Husb's Age: 27 Wife's Age: 16 Husb's Cond: single Wife's Cond: single Husb Born: Campbell Co Va Wife Born: Campbell Co Va Husb's Res: Campbell Co Va Wife's Res: Campbell Co Va Husb's Par: Thomas & Betsey Ann Wright Wife's Par: Tymothy & Mary A Trent Husb's Occ: Farming Minister: S. J. Liggan	Benjamin F. Wright, son of 1882 Thomas B. Wright of Campbell County and grandson of Thomas Wright of (Campbell County)
02	077	1885/12/23	James W. Frieman & Betty Wright	Col: Colored Husb's Age: 21 Wife's Age: 22 Husb's Cond: Single Wife's Cond: Single Minister: H. Stephenson	
02	079	1886/12/23	Jonathan O. Dudley & Mary E. Wright	Place: Campbell Co Ho Va Col: White Husb's Age: 26 Wife's Age: 17 Husb's Cond: single Wife's Cond: single Husb Born: Campbell Co Va Wife Born: Pittsylvania Co Va Husb's Res: Campbell Co Va Wife's Res: Campbell Co Va Husb's Par: Jno & Henrietta Dudley Wife's Par: Robt J & Louisa Wright Husb's Occ: Farmer Minister: Wm. E. Payne	Mary E. (Wright) Dudley, daughter of Robert J. Wright

Book/Page	Date	Names	Other Information	Identification
02 140	1889/04/24	Frank Goff & Blanche E. Wright	Place: Campbell Co Va Col: White Husb's Age: 31 Wife's Age: 28 Husb's Cond: single Wife's Cond: widowed Husb Born: Campbell Co Va Wife Born: Campbell Co Va Husb's Res: Campbell Co Va Wife's Res: Campbell Co Va Husb's Par: Chas & Mary A Wife's Par: Thos D & E A Husb's Occ: Farmer Minister: J. S. Mason	Blanche E. (Cardwell) Wright, widow of Jessie H. Wright, a son of 1873 John Patterson Wright of Campbell County, grandson of 1811 John Wright of Campbell County, and great grandson of Robert Wright, Sr. (Campbell County)
02 133	1891/10/25	Edward Wright & Annie Melton	Place: Campbell Co Va Col: White Husb's Age: 21 Wife's Age: 17 Husb's Cond: Single Wife's Cond: Single Husb Born: Campbell Co Va Wife Born: Campbell Co Va Husb's Res: Campbell Co Va Wife's Res: Campbell Co Va Husb's Par: John & Sallie Wright Wife's Par: Alex & Bettie Melton Husb's Occ: Labourer Minister: C. E. Watts	Edward Sylvanus Wright, son of John H. Wright, grandson of 1882 Thomas B. Wright of Campbell County, and great grandson of Thomas Wright (Campbell County)

Appendix: Campbell County, Virginia, Marriage Records

Book/Page		Date	Names	Other Information	Identification
03	001	1893/10/04	Henry Wright & Kitty Shelton	Place: Campbell Co Va Col: Colored Husb's Age: 60 Wife's Age: 53 Husb's Cond: widowed Wife's Cond: widowed Husb Born: Amherst Co Va Wife Born: Campbell Co Va Husb's Res: Campbell Co Va Wife's Res: Campbell Co Va Husb's Par: Senid(?) & Jane Wife's par: Husb's Occ: Farmer Minister: Jas. B. Shelton	Henry Wright, son of Senid(?) Wright
03	008	1895/08/22	W. B. Wright & Mary E. Farmer	Place: Campbell Co. Va. Col: White Husb's Age: 25 Wife's Age: 23 Husb's Cond: Single Wife's Cond: Single Husb Born: Campbell Co. Va Wife Born: Campbell Co. Va Husb's Res: Campbell Co. Va Wife's Res: Campbell Co. Va Husb's Par: Richd & Justina Wright Wife's Par: Wm H & Martha D Farmer Husb's Occ: Farmer Minister: A. F. Rachal	William T. or B. Wright, son of William Richard Wright, grandson of 1882 Thomas B. Wright of Campbell County, and great grandson of Thomas Wright (Campbell County)

Appendix: Campbell County, Virginia, Marriage Records

Book/Page	Date	Names	Other Information	Identification
03 011	1896/03/04	James Wright & Bertha Irvine	Place: Campbell Co. Va Col: Cold Husb's Age: 22 yrs 11 mo & 21 days Wife's Age: 21 yrs & 3 days Husb's Cond: Single Wife's Cond: Single Husb Born: Campbell Co Va Wife Born: Campbell Co Va Husb's Res: Campbell Co Va Wife's Res: Campbell Co Va Husb's Par: Nelson & Sarah Wright Wife's Par: Wm & Annie Irvine Husb's Occ: Laborer Minister: C. A. Smith	James Wright, son of Nelson Wright
03 013	1896/12/19	Grant Wright & Tamar Payne	Place: Campbell County Virginia Color: Colored Husb's Age: 25 Wife's Age: 22 Husb's Cond: Single Wife's Cond: Single Husb Born: Pittsylvania County Virginia Wife Born: Campbell County Virginia Husb's Res: Campbell County Virginia Wife's Res: Campbell County Virginia Husb's Par: Frank & Louisa Wright Wife's Par: Milie Payne & __ Husb's Occ: Blacksmith Minister: J. T. Settle	Grant Wright, son of Frank Wright

Book/Page	Date	Names	Other Information	Identification
03 020	1898/09/25	David L. Wright & M. V. Pettigrew	Place: Campbell Co. Va Col: White Husb's Age: 50 Wife's Age: 40 Husb's Cond: widowed Wife's Cond: Single Husb Born: Appomattox Wife Born: Campbell Co. Va. Husb's Res: Campbell Co. Va. Wife's Res: Campbell Co. Va. Husb's Par: J. P. & Elizabeth Wright Wife's Par: J. W. & Mary Pettigrew Husb's Occ: Carpenter Minister: J. T. Thornhill	David Luther Wright, son of 1873 John Patterson Wright of Campbell County, grandson of 1811 John Wright of Campbell County, and great grandson of Robert Wright, Sr. (Campbell County)
03 024	1899/09/06	Adlophus Humbler & Celinda Wright	Place: Campbell Co. Va. Color: Colored Husb's Age: 22 Wife's Age: 18 Husb's Cond: Single Wife's Cond: Single Husb Born: Campbell Co. Va. Wife Born: Campbell Co. Va. Husb's Res: Campbell Co. Va. Wife's Res: Campbell Co. Va. Husb's Par: Adolphus & Rosa Humbles Wife's Par: Ben. & Mollie Wright Husb's Occ: Farming Minister: Edward Staples	Celinda (Wright) Humbler, daughter of Benjamin Wright

Book/Page	Date	Names	Other Information	Identification
03 028	1900/08/12	Letcher Almond & Gracie Wright	Place: Campbell Co. Va. Col: White Husb's Age: 22 Wife's Age: 21 Husb's Cond: Single Wife's Cond: Single Husb Born: Campbell Co Va. Wife Born: Campbell Co Va. Husb's Res: Campbell Co Va. Wife's Res: Campbell Co Va. Husb's Par: Barney & Christiana Wife's Par: James R. & Jane R. Husb's Occ: R.R. Employee Minister: S. J. Liggan	Grace T. (Wright) Almond, daughter of James Robert Wright, granddaughter of 1882 Thomas B. Wright of Campbell County, and great granddaughter of Thomas Wright (Campbell County)
03 029	1900/09/05	John Richard Duffey & Hattie M. Wright	Place: Campbell Co. Va. Col: White Husb's Age: 22 Wife's Age: 22 Husb's Cond: single Wife's Cond: single Husb Born: Pittsylvania Co Va Wife Born: Campbell Co Va Husb's Res: Canterburry W. Va. Wife's Res: Campbell Co. Va. Husb's Par: Nicholas & Ida Duffey Wife's Par: Thos T. Wright & Roberta Wright Husb's Occ: R.R. Sec. fireman Minister: C. H. Gallaway	Hattie M. (Wright) Duffey, daughter of Thomas Turner Wright, granddaughter of 1883 Thomas Smith Wright of Campbell County, and great granddaughter of 1842 Thomas Wright of Buckingham County

Appendix: Campbell County, Virginia, Marriage Records

Book/Page	Date	Names	Other Information	Identification
03 030	1900/11/28	Beauregard Wright & Harriet Stewart	Place: Campbell Co. Va. Color: Colored Husb's Age: 36 Wife's Age: 29 Husb's Cond: Widowed Wife's Cond: Widowed Husb Born: Appomattox Co. Va. Wife Born: Buckingham Co. Va. Husb's Res: Campbell Co. Va. Wife's Res: Campbell Co. Va. Husb's Par: Nat & Malinda Wife's Par: Elijah & Judie Banks Husb's Occ: Miller Minister: S. A. Garland	Beauregard Wright, son of Nat Wright

INDEX

Pettigrew, Mary, 19
Pettigrew, Mary H, 8
Plunkett, Mildred, 2
Rachal, A. F., 17
Rector, John, 1
Rodes, Jno. T., 14
Settle, J. T., 18
Shelton, Jas. B., 17
Shelton, Kitty, 17
Smith, Amanda, 4
Smith, C. A., 18
Smith, Nancy, 6
Smith, Paschal B, 6
Smith, Paschel, 4
Spriggs, Joseph, 6, 7
Staples, Edward, 19
Staples, Frances, 1
Stephenson, H., 15
Stewart, Harriet, 21
Stratton, Daniel, 2, 3
Tate, Bell, 13
Thornhill, J. T., 12, 19
Trent, Grace, 14
Trent, Jane T. R. H., 14
Trent, Mary A, 15
Trent, Sarah E., 15
Trent, Tazwell, 14
Trent, Tymothy, 15
Turner, James, 2
Turner, John, 3
Turner, Leonard, 3
Turner, Mariah, 3
Tweedy, Jr., Joseph, 2
Walker, Jr., John, 2
Walthall, Amanda M., 5
Walthall, Betsy Ann, 5
Walthall, Robert, 5
Watts, C. E., 16
Williams, A. C, 12
Williams, J A., 12
Williams, John C., 12

Williams, Mary L., 3
Williams, William, 3
Williamson, Archer, 2
Williamson, Henry, 1
Wilson, Elizabeth, 3
Wilson, John, 3
Wilson, Peter H., 3
Wood, Elizabeth A., 3
Wood, James A., 7
Wood, Joseph, 3
Wood, Martha A, 7
Wood, Wm B., 7
Woodall, Cyrus, 9
Woodall, Elizabeth, 9
Woodall, Samuel F., 9
Woods, Benj, 7
Woodson, Thomas A., 3
Wright, Agnes, 2
Wright, Anny, 1
Wright, Beauregard, 21
Wright, Ben., 19
Wright, Benj. P., 7
Wright, Benjamin F., 15
Wright, Betsey Ann, 15
Wright, Betsy, 10
Wright, Betsy A., 7
Wright, Betsy Ann, 10, 11, 14
Wright, Bettie E., 9
Wright, Betty, 15
Wright, Blanche E., 16
Wright, C. S., 12
Wright, Camden G., 4
Wright, Campbell S., 4
Wright, Catharine R., 7
Wright, Celinda, 19
Wright, Charles, 1, 2
Wright, Chas., 2
Wright, Daniel P., 2
Wright, Daniel P., 8
Wright, Danl, 8
Wright, David L., 19

Wright, E A, 16
Wright, Edward, 16
Wright, Elifat, 9
Wright, Elijah A., 3
Wright, Elisha F., 4
Wright, Eliz., 8
Wright, Eliza, 2, 6
Wright, Elizabeth, 1, 2, 5, 6, 8, 9, 11, 13, 19
Wright, Elizabeth F., 10
Wright, Elizabith, 14
Wright, Ellen, 5
Wright, F. K., 14
Wright, Frank, 18
Wright, George, 1, 2
Wright, George A., 2, 4
Wright, Gracie, 20
Wright, Grant, 18
Wright, Hattie M., 20
Wright, Henry, 17
Wright, J. P., 9, 19
Wright, James, 12, 18
Wright, James A, 13
Wright, James R., 11, 20
Wright, James Robert, 14
Wright, James W., 5
Wright, Jane, 17
Wright, Jane R., 20
Wright, Jesse H., 13
Wright, Jno P, 11
Wright, John, 1
Wright, John, 16
Wright, John B., 4
Wright, John H., 3
Wright, John J., 7
Wright, John P., 2, 4, 5, 10, 13
Wright, John W., 12
Wright, Justina, 17
Wright, Lewis, 5
Wright, Louisa, 15, 18
Wright, Lovin A., 4

Wright, Lucinda, 3
Wright, Lucinda P., 3
Wright, M. A., 12
Wright, Malinda, 21
Wright, Mary A., 6, 11
Wright, Mary E., 15
Wright, Meredith P., 3
Wright, Mollie, 19
Wright, Nannie J., 12
Wright, Nannie M., 5
Wright, Nat, 21
Wright, Nelson, 18
Wright, Parker A., 3
Wright, Paulina P., 8
Wright, Polly, 2
Wright, Price, 7
Wright, Pryor, 3
Wright, Pryor B., 3
Wright, Richd, 17
Wright, Rob, 2
Wright, Robert, 1, 2
Wright, Sr., Robert, 2
Wright, Robert, 5
Wright, Roberta, 20
Wright, Robert B., 4
Wright, Robert C., 3
Wright, Robert D., 5
Wright, Robert J., 4
Wright, Robt J, 15
Wright, Sallie, 9, 16
Wright, Sally, 2
Wright, Samuel A., 10
Wright, Sarah, 7, 18
Wright, Sarah E., 4
Wright, Senid(?), 17
Wright, Shelton, 8
Wright, Susan, 12
Wright, Susanna, 1
Wright, Sylvia, 2
Wright, Tho. B., 6
Wright, Thomas, 15

Wright, Thomas B., 3
Wright, Thos, 14
Wright, Thos B., 7, 10, 11
Wright, Thos D, 16
Wright, Thos S., 14
Wright, Thos T., 20
Wright, W. B., 17
Wright, W. H., 8
Wright, William, 12
Wright, William P., 2
Wright, William R., 6
Wright, Wilson, 3
Wright, Wm. M., 4
Wright, Wm. P., 14
Wrights, J. P., 9

Other Heritage Books by Robert N. Grant

Identifying the Wrights in the Goochland County, Virginia Tithe Lists, 1732-84

The Identification of 1809 William Wright of Franklin County, Virginia, as the Son of 1792 John Wright of Fauquier County, Virginia, and Elizabeth (Bronaugh) (Darnall) Wright

Wright Family Birth Records (1853-1896) and Marriage Records (1788-1915): Franklin County, Virginia, 1853-1896

Wright Family Birth Records, 1853-1896; Marriage Records, 1761-1900; Census Records, 1810-1900, in Amherst County, Virginia

Wright Family Birth Records, 1853-1896; Marriage Records, 1808-1910; Census Records, 1810-1900; Patent Deeds and Land Grants; Deed Records, 1808-1910; Death Records, 1853-1896; Probate Records, 1808-1900, in Nelson County, Virginia

Wright Family Birth Records, 1853–1896; Marriage Records, 1777–1918; Census Records, 1810–1900; Deed Records, 1777–1902; Death Records, 1853–1896; Cemetery Records, and Probate Records, 1777–1909; in Rockbridge County, Virginia

Wright Family Birth Records (1853-1896) and Marriage Records (1782-1900): Campbell County, Virginia

Wright Family Birth Records, Marriage Records, and Personal Property Tax Lists: Appomattox County, Virginia

Wright Family Census Records, Deed Records, Land Tax Lists, Death Records and Probate Records: Appomattox County, Virginia

Wright Family Census Records: Bedford County, Virginia, 1810-1900

Wright Family Census Records: Campbell County, Virginia, 1810-1900

Wright Family Census Records: Franklin County, Virginia, 1810-1900

Wright Family Death Records (1853-1920), Cemetery Records by Cemetery, and Probate Records (1782-1900): Campbell County, Virginia

Wright Family Death Records (1854-1920), Cemetery Records by Cemetery, and Probate Records (1785-1928): Franklin County, Virginia

Wright Family Death, Cemetery and Probate Records: Bedford County, Virginia

Wright Family Deed Records (1782-1900) and Land Tax List (1782-1850): Campbell County, Virginia

Wright Family Land Grants (1785-1900) and Deed Records (1785-1897): Franklin County, Virginia

Wright Family Land Grants, Deed Records, Land Tax List, Death Records, Probate Records: Prince Edward County, Virginia

Wright Family Land Records: Bedford County, Virginia

Wright Family Land Tax Lists: Franklin County, Virginia, 1786-1860

Wright Family Land Tax Lists: Rockbridge County, Virginia, 1782-1850

Wright Family Land Tax Records: Amherst County, Virginia, 1782-1850

Wright Family Land Tax Records: Nelson County, Virginia, 1809-1850

Wright Family Patent Deeds and Land Grants, 1761-1900, Deed Records, 1761-1903; Chancery Court Files, 1804-1900; Death Records, 1853-1920; Cemetery Records by Cemetery; and Probate Records, 1761-1900, in Amherst County, Virginia

Wright Family Personal Property Tax Lists: Amherst County, Virginia, 1782-1850

Wright Family Personal Property Tax Lists: Campbell County, Virginia, 1785-1850

Wright Family Personal Property Tax Lists: Franklin County, Virginia, 1786-1850

Wright Family Personal Property Tax Lists: Nelson County, Virginia, 1809-1850

Wright Family Personal Property Tax Lists: Rockbridge County, Virginia, 1782-1850

Wright Family Personal Property Tax Records for Bedford County, Virginia, 1782 to 1850

Wright Family Records: Births in Bedford County, Virginia